Build a Culture You Don't Lose

The Turnover Signal Model™: A Practical Guide to Assessing, Understanding, and Redesigning the Systems People Leave Behind

Author: Dr. Ashlyn Daniels

For permissions, inquiries, or speaking engagements,
please contact:
SigTacTure@yahoo.com

First Edition, 2025
ISBN: 979-8-218-75243-9

Cover design by Dr. Ashlyn Daniels

Published in the United States by Dr. Ashlyn Daniels
Printed in the United States of America

Dedication

To my parents, thank you for giving me the freedom to lead, create, and rise. You didn't just give me life, you breathed it back into me when I needed it most. You are my heroes, and the example you've set is my compass.

To my husband, your love steadied me through late nights and uncertain seasons. Thank you for being my rock, my safe place, and the one who never tires of my ideas or my doubts.

To my daughter, may this achievement show you what's possible when passion meets persistence. May you chase bold dreams and know that difficulty doesn't diminish destiny; it defines it.

To my grandma, your voice and belief have been etched into my soul. Your calls, your kindness, and your strength have shaped who I am and carried me through.

And to my grandfather, though you now rest in glory, I hear your laughter and encouragement still. Thank you for challenging me early on and cheering me on from heaven. This one's for you.

Preface: The Spark of The Signal

The idea for this book began with tension. Tension between leadership intentions and employee realities. Between what turnover metrics capture and what truly disappears when a colleague walks away. Turnover is usually framed as an HR number, but behind every exit is a story that metrics miss. What really disappears? Knowledge. Trust. Customer relationships. Continuity.

During my doctoral research, I focused on those who remain after others leave. The employees weren't just holding the line; they were carrying the emotional, cultural, and operational weight of the organization in silence. They held the wisdom that no system was asking for.

Turnover, I realized, is often treated as a symptom, something to fix or prevent. Still, every exit is a **signal**, a signal of organizational strain, of leadership misalignment, of cultural erosion, or knowledge fragility. When someone leaves, what's left behind tells us everything we need to know, if we're willing to listen.

As I conducted interviews and gathered stories for my dissertation, employees talked about grief, guilt, burnout, and the unspoken emotional toll of onboarding new hires without guidance. They spoke about being promoted without support and about leaders doing their best but lacking the tools to navigate disruption.

Some organizations tried to recover with checklists or quick fixes. Others moved on without acknowledging the impact, but in nearly every story, the same message came through: no one was tending to the people who stayed.

Turnover metrics are often only the tip of the iceberg. What lies beneath the surface, the unspoken knowledge, the emotional strain, and the subtle shifts in trust and rhythm. What you don't see is where the real story is told. Like an iceberg, most of what shapes an organization remains hidden unless we are willing to look below the surface.

That's when I created **The Turnover Signal Model™**, a systems-based framework that views turnover not as an endpoint, but as a diagnostic opportunity, a way to explore what's left, what's fragile, and what needs redesigning. The model applies **Human and Organizational Performance (HOP)** and **Multicausal Root Cause Analysis (MRCA)** to move away from blame and toward insight. It centers the thoughts, needs, and adaptations of the people still there, the ones who feel the impact most deeply.

This book blends research, reflection, and lived experience. It doesn't offer quick fixes. It provides patterns, frameworks, and honest stories from across industries. Leadership here isn't about charisma. It's about courage. Culture isn't assumed; it's engineered, and retention isn't a benefit; it's a design outcome.

If you're leading through disruption, this book will challenge you to look differently at what's leaving and what's left behind.

By Dr. Ashlyn Daniels
July 2025

Part I: Signals in the Silence

When I began my doctorate, I knew I'd need a dissertation topic. I kept circling back to that tension, the thing no one was talking about. I'd seen it play out over and over again: people left, systems collapsed, customers were affected, knowledge evaporated, and the people who stayed were left holding it all together.

I wanted to do more than tell a story. I wanted to **prove** it.

During my time in hospital billing, I was honored with the *Leaders of Tomorrow Award*. After two years of coming close, I was finally selected. In the interviews, they asked: "What's the difference between management and leadership?" That question stuck with me, not because I had the perfect answer, but because I had to **become** the answer.

I realized that what I wanted wasn't a title, it was **impact**. I wanted to lead in a way that made people feel safe, supported, and seen. I wanted to improve systems, so people had what they needed to succeed.

Then came the hard lesson.

After being promoted to supervisor, I followed the onboarding advice I was given: shadow your peers, do what they do, and figure it out as you go. I did just that, and still, I was put on a final written warning for the same practices my peers used, and then I was let go. Not for misconduct, for doing what the broken system allowed and modeled.

At a **Human and Organizational Performance (HOP) Summit in July 2025**, Dr. Ben Goodheart said something that reframed it all for me. I'm paraphrasing, but the message was this:

"When someone is promoted, they often take with them the operational knowledge no one captured, and they enter leadership without the support or development they truly need. Emotional intelligence, coaching, system thinking, none of it is handed to them."

That moment made me revisit everything. What had failed wasn't just me; it was the **system** that promoted me without a map, without mentorship, without structure.

Not Just a Hunch

Not every experience I had was bad. I've worked under some incredible leaders and some toxic ones. If you've never had to recover from bad leadership, count yourself lucky. If you have, you understand the weight of what I'm describing.

I've worked in a wide range of industries, from healthcare, retail, fitness, manufacturing, and tech, and every role, one word followed me: **turnover**. Voluntary turnover, to be exact. The kind where someone chooses to leave, and you're left with more questions than answers.

I remember that sinking feeling whenever a teammate left. Not just the sadness, the dread, the knowing that their responsibilities would likely fall to me, with no raise, no restructuring, and no roadmap. It would be at least 3 to 9 months before someone new came in, and by then, we'd be patching gaps, not building systems. Sometimes, the organization responded with care, but often, it responded with indifference, avoidance, or an empty process.

Customer satisfaction has always mattered to me. Without customers, there is no job, and yet, many organizations treat customer-facing roles as interchangeable, disposable.

When someone leaves, the knowledge of that customer leaves with them, and trust fractures. Over time, I noticed that turnover wasn't just hurting teams, it was damaging **customer satisfaction** too.

I had a hunch there was a connection between turnover, knowledge loss, and service decline, but it was just that: a gut feeling. All of my experiences and hunches led me to my research: **The Effects of Employee Turnover on Customer Satisfaction and Knowledge Loss.** My findings validated what I had felt for years, and they revealed new insights I hadn't considered.

If you've made it this far, keep reading!

This book will guide you through the signals beneath turnover, the patterns, pain points, and potential it reveals. Not just about those who leave, but about the systems they leave behind. Using the Turnover Signal Model™, you'll learn how to decode disruption, center the experiences of those who stay, and design cultures worth keeping.

Turnover isn't just a logistical event. It's a **cultural signal,** and far too often, organizations ignore what it's trying to tell them.

The Silent Drain

Turnover often hides its most damaging effects beneath the surface. Leaders see the immediate, visible costs, such as recruitment fees, onboarding time, and a temporary decline in productivity while new hires adjust. Far less obvious are the slow leaks in knowledge, trust, and capacity that occur long before anyone leaves.

The drain begins quietly. A skilled employee takes on more responsibilities to cover for a teammate who is struggling or absent. Documentation is postponed in favor of urgent deadlines. Minor errors multiply because fewer people remember the original processes. Over time, these gaps compound, making daily work more difficult for everyone. Morale erodes in subtle ways. Remaining employees notice when their extra efforts go unacknowledged or when leadership minimizes the strain. Trust begins to weaken as workloads feel less fair and communication becomes reactive. The team's rhythm changes, and collaboration feels heavier, even if no one can point to a single incident that caused it.

Financial losses grow in the background. Repeated mistakes lead to rework, and delays create missed opportunities. Service quality may dip, which erodes client confidence and damages the organization's reputation. These costs rarely appear on a balance sheet until a crisis forces attention, yet they are as real as any direct expense.

The most significant damage occurs when leaders misread stability as strength. A team can appear steady while already absorbing the effects of burnout, misalignment, or fractured communication. When departure finally happens, the underlying cracks widen quickly, exposing how much the organization relied on hidden effort.

The silent drain is preventable. Detecting early warning signs, understanding where systems are fragile, and acting before the loss of talent is the only option to stop the quiet leak before it becomes a flood. The Turnover Signal Model™ exists to make those warning signs visible and to help leaders respond in time to protect both culture and performance.

When Engagement Scores Lie

Positive engagement survey results can hide serious problems. Leaders often interpret high scores as proof of a healthy culture, believing the numbers confirm that people feel valued, supported, and committed. In reality, survey responses often reflect only part of the truth, and sometimes they tell a story designed to protect employees rather than inform leadership.

Fear of retaliation shapes many survey results. Employees who have witnessed negative consequences for speaking honestly may choose to give favorable ratings despite their experience. The goal becomes self-preservation, not transparency. Even anonymous surveys cannot entirely remove the pressure when people suspect their feedback could be traced back to them.

Some teams feel collective pressure to present a united front. They may avoid admitting problems in writing to protect their department's reputation, especially if leadership compares results across teams. The decisions for a united front create a culture of silence where the image of harmony matters more than addressing the underlying issues.

Survey design also plays a role in creating a false sense of health. Questions that focus on satisfaction rather than on system effectiveness fail to uncover the structural issues that drive disengagement and turnover. A team might report feeling satisfied in the short term while quietly managing broken processes or unclear expectations that will cause long-term damage.

Leaders who rely solely on engagement scores risk missing the deeper patterns that predict turnover. Real cultural health is not measured by temporary morale but by the organization's ability to maintain clarity, trust, and support even during change or challenge. Without tools that reveal these conditions, problems remain hidden until turnover forces them into view.

The Turnover Signal Model™ addresses this gap by focusing on system health rather than sentiment. It uses signals that appear in daily operations and relationships, which selective survey responses cannot mask. This approach allows leaders to see the early warnings that engagement surveys often fail to detect.

Leader Fatigue and the Fragile Culture

Leaders are not immune to the hidden costs of turnover and strain. Many enter the role with a commitment to guiding teams through challenges, only to discover that the real test is sustaining their energy while doing so. Fatigue sets in when the demands of managing daily operations collide with the responsibility of protecting culture.

Minor signs of leader fatigue often go unnoticed at first. Meetings feel more like obligations than opportunities for connection. Decisions take longer because the mental space for strategic thinking has been replaced by a cycle of urgent problem-solving. Leaders spend more time reacting than anticipating, leaving little capacity for building trust or improving systems.

As energy drains, so does cultural resilience. Leaders under constant strain may default to quick fixes that keep work moving but leave underlying issues unresolved. A decision to delay addressing conflict, skip a coaching conversation, or postpone a process review may seem minor in the moment. Repeated over time, such choices create an environment where cracks deepen unnoticed.

Leader fatigue also affects how feedback is received. A worn-down leader may interpret concerns as complaints, dismissing them rather than seeing them as signals worth addressing. This reaction discourages honesty and reinforces a culture of silence. The result is a team that learns to work around problems instead of solving them.

Fragility spreads quickly in cultures where leadership energy is depleted. Trust weakens when employees sense disengagement from their leaders. Systems lose reliability as oversight declines. Service quality suffers when leaders no longer have the bandwidth to ensure alignment across teams. Protecting culture requires protecting the people responsible for leading it. Leaders must have the tools, support, and space to maintain clarity, trust, and stability. Without this foundation, even the most dedicated leader cannot prevent the culture from becoming fragile. The Turnover Signal Model™ offers a structure that helps leaders identify strain early, share the responsibility for cultural health, and prevent the slow erosion that fatigue creates.

Part II: The Turnover Signal Model™

When someone leaves a team, it creates more than a vacancy. It often sets off a series of disruptions, some obvious, others hidden beneath the surface. Every exit is not just the visible moment of someone leaving; the exit is the tip of the iceberg. Beneath the surface are hidden disruptions: undocumented knowledge, fractured trust, and emotional weight that rarely make it into metrics but carry lasting impact. The immediate response might involve backfilling a position or redistributing tasks. Over time, more profound consequences begin to unfold: delays in decision-making, confusion in handoffs, emotional strain among team members, or drops in service quality. These are not just the results of someone leaving; they are signals from the system itself.

Too often, organizations treat turnover as a human resources issue or an individual event, but what if the real opportunity lies not in replacing the person who left, but in learning what their absence reveals? What if each departure was a chance to see how the organization truly functions and where it quietly struggles?

The Turnover Signal Model™ was created to help leaders and teams do just that by providing a structured way to identify and interpret the patterns

that emerge when someone leaves. More importantly, it offers a
proactive approach for identifying those same patterns before turnover occurs because the strongest organizations don't just respond to exits, they prepare for them by building systems that can adapt, absorb, and evolve.

Creating The Turnover Signal Model™

In my doctoral project, I didn't analyze metrics. I studied lived experience, the emotional and operational ripple effects of employee turnover. I interviewed people across industries who stayed after teammates, leaders, and culture-carriers walked out the door.

Three research questions aligned with the foundation of my doctoral project:

RQ1: What are the lived experiences of employees facing workplace turnover?

RQ2: How do employees' perceptions of turnover affect customer service quality?

RQ3: What strategies do employees use to improve customer satisfaction post-turnover?

The **Turnover Signal Model™** emerged from eight recurring patterns identified in interview transcripts, patterns that reflected not complaints, but systemic truths. The insights became the foundation for what I now call **Turnover Signals™**, later explained in the book.

The Turnover Signal Model™ isn't theory. It's a codified truth from those who were often unheard. This book exists to give voice to their insights and to give you tools to lead differently.

From Research to Turnover Signals™

The insights came directly from people, not from reports. Interview participants described turnover not in exit data or dashboards, but in missing rhythms, dropped handoffs, and invisible strain. I realized then that turnover was not just a moment. It was a message.

The stories revealed patterns. Patterns shaped themes. Themes evolved into what is now the Turnover Signal Model™, a structured way to spot system strain by paying attention to what the people who remain are carrying.

The chart below shows how the research themes transformed into the eight Turnover Signals™:

Research Theme	Turnover Signal™
Lack of formal knowledge transfer structures	**Undocumented Knowledge Gaps Emerge**
Specialized and tacit knowledge is hard to replace	**Tacit Rhythm Disappears**
Emotional impact of turnover	**Emotional Burden Goes Unnoticed**
Loss of relationship continuity with clients	**Client Trust Fractures**
Decreased service quality during transitions	**Service Quality Suffers**
Culture and leadership matter more than pay	**Culture & Leadership Gaps Show**
Weak systems, training, and cross-coverage compound risk	**Broken Systems**
Cross-cutting organizational challenges (e.g., unclear roles)	**Cross-Org Misalignment Surfaces**

Each signal tells a systemic story rather than presenting a simple symptom. Turnover Signals™ are not one-time issues; they repeat and speak loudly when leaders choose to listen.

In the chapters ahead, you will see how the Turnover Signal Model™ helps you:

- Recognize what each signal looks like in action
- Understand why it happens beneath the surface
- Interpret the message each signal carries
- Respond in ways that build trust and resilience

The opportunity ahead is to decode disruption and design what comes next.

Let us begin not with who left, but with what they left behind.

The Four-Step Practice

The Turnover Signal Model™ is both a diagnostic framework and a design approach. It helps teams see what is typically invisible: weak points, unspoken burdens, and systems that rely too heavily on individual memory or goodwill.

The Turnover Signal Model™ follows a clear four-step cycle: Assess, Understand, Redesign, and Sustain. Each step builds on the one before, creating a rhythm of inquiry and adaptation. The visual below illustrates how to move from noticing patterns to embedding changes that last.

Assess
Identify active signals and areas of fragility

Four-Step Practice
for the Turnover Signal Model

Understand
Document examples and pinpoint causes

Redesign
Change expectations or systems

Substain
Regularly use the model for learning

The Four Step Practice anchors the Turnover Signal Model™ as a practical and repeatable discipline, encouraging teams to learn from disruption and redesign with intention.

The practices function as part of a continuous cycle, repeated across teams, transitions, and seasons of change.

The model also provides tools, which will be explored in depth in the following sections.
The tools work together in a flow rather than in isolation. Adopting them as a regular practice makes the model both actionable and sustainable, rather than a one-time response.

Not Just An After-Turnover Tool

While the model was initially developed by studying the aftermath of turnover, it proves equally powerful and often more impactful when applied proactively.

Turnover may be the moment that draws attention to a problem, yet the signals usually surface long before someone walks out the door. Signals emerge in misaligned workflows, overstretched teams, unspoken norms, and the gradual erosion of trust. They accumulate quietly but persistently.

The model serves as more than a post-mortem tool. It operates as a health check, a mirror, and a way to recognize what a system already knows but has not yet articulated.

Use it before turnover happens:
- Conduct proactive system audits
- Identify signals before they solidify into problems
- Strengthen culture, clarity, and continuity across teams

Signals remain active even without turnover; they require awareness. Applying the model in steady times, not only in response to disruption, develops the capacity for sustainable performance.

The Shift

By the time someone leaves, the visible disruption is only the tip of the iceberg. What was long accumulating beneath the surface finally became impossible to ignore. Turnover is not the beginning of disruption; it marks the moment disruption can no longer be ignored. Listening earlier allows leaders to act earlier, spotting signs of emotional strain, clarifying hidden expectations, and protecting team flow before pressure causes collapse.

Examples of what may surface include:

- A team silently absorbing extra workload after a change
- A client experiencing uncertainty when a key contact transitions out
- A new hire is struggling to learn "how we work" because tacit knowledge was not shared

Formal resignations are not required for these signals to be real. The model helps identify, name, and address them before they escalate into costly problems.

Over time, the Turnover Signal Model™ evolves from a diagnostic tool into a discipline. It becomes a way of paying attention and building a culture that absorbs loss, learns from disruption, and adapts in real time.

The strongest teams are not defined by retaining every individual. They are characterized by their response when someone leaves and by whether the system continues with clarity, confidence, and care.

The Turnover Signal Model™ provides this readiness. It enables the shift from reaction to redesign, from silence to sensemaking, and from turnover as disruption to turnover as insight.

Culture is not built only when someone joins; it is revealed in how the team responds when someone departs and in how the organization grows from that moment.

With the origin and purpose of the Turnover Signal Model™ established, the next step is application. The model is more than a theory; it is a practice supported by tools that help assess, understand, and strengthen organizations. Whether facing a recent departure or proactively designing for resilience, these tools guide leaders to listen to their systems and act with intention.

The chapters ahead introduce the Turnover Signal Self-Assessment™ and the SigTac Signal™ Tool. Together, they move you from insight to redesign and from uncertainty to clarity. They not only reveal what is already straining your system but also spark meaningful change before that strain becomes a crisis.

Part III: The Turnover Signals™

Before exploring each of the eight signals, it is essential to understand how they currently appear within your organization. The Turnover Signal Self-Assessment™ is designed to reveal these patterns in a way that connects daily operations to long-term cultural health.

The Turnover Signal Wheel™ provides the visual framework for the model. Each of the eight signals sits within one of four essential domains of organizational health and resilience: Clarity & Continuity, Trust & Team Health, Systems & Support, and Service & Impact.

The Turnover Signal Wheel™

At the center of the Wheel is **Psychological Safety**, the condition that allows every signal to surface honestly and be addressed constructively. Without it, even the most accurate tool will struggle to uncover the truth.

The Self-Assessment is built around these eight core signals across the four domains. Your responses indicate which signals are already active, where invisible strain may be accumulating, and which areas of your system require the most immediate attention. By anchoring the assessment in these domains, you are not simply rating sentiment; you are mapping the health of your systems in a way that allows for targeted, lasting improvements.

Now, let's explore **The Turnover Signals™**.

Domain 1: Clarity & Continuity

Clarity ensures that everyone understands what must be done, why it matters, and how to carry it out. Continuity preserves that clarity over time so that the organization can function smoothly even when people or circumstances change. Without both, even highly skilled teams lose alignment and waste valuable energy.

Turnover often exposes weaknesses in this domain first. Knowledge gaps appear when key processes, contacts, or decisions live only in someone's memory. The rhythm of work falters when departures, absences, or role changes disrupt unspoken routines. Inconsistent communication or undocumented workflows force teams to reinvent steps that should already be clear.

Signals in this domain: **Undocumented Knowledge Gaps Emerge** and **Tacit Rhythm Disappears**, reveal where the organization's foundation is vulnerable. These signals do not just indicate poor recordkeeping or lost efficiency; they point to deeper risks that can multiply if left unaddressed. By strengthening clarity and continuity, leaders reduce dependence on individual memory, maintain operational flow, and protect the organization from instability during change.

Undocumented Knowledge Gaps Emerge Signal

Every organization relies on knowledge to function: how things are done, where important resources live, who to ask for help, and what to avoid. Not all of this knowledge is written down. A signal appears when critical information exists only in people's heads rather than in shared systems. When a team member leaves and others cannot access their knowledge, progress slows, mistakes multiply, and decision-making suffers.

The issue extends beyond documentation; it threatens continuity and resilience. A team that cannot operate effectively without one person is too fragile. This signal calls for examining where knowledge lives, how accessible it is, and what must change so work can continue smoothly regardless of who is present.

Ask yourself: When was the last time your team got stuck because no one could find the answer? What did that reveal about where knowledge truly lives? Remember, "Just ask so-and-so" is not a process. It is a warning.

When an employee departs, they take more than their login credentials and job title. Often, they take the operating manual that exists only in their head. What remains is not simply an empty chair or inbox. What remains is confusion. Teams are left asking: Who owns this process now? Why was it done that way? Where is the real version of that file, not the outdated one in the shared drive?

The first turnover signal appears quietly but carries weight. It becomes clear when slack threads go unanswered, when new hires repeat mistakes that could have been prevented, or when people spend half a day tracking down information someone used to know by heart. These are not minor inconveniences. They are symptoms of a system that never captured its wisdom.

Picture your team trying to run a core process once owned by a departing employee. The documentation is outdated, scattered, or vague. No one fully understands why specific steps exist or how they interact. People improvise, processes break, and a frustrated client calls to ask why something slipped. In that moment, the cost of undocumented knowledge becomes painfully clear.

Bold truth: You did not just lose an employee. You lost logic. You lost your memory. You lost fluency.

Documentation Isn't About Volume
Creating a massive SOP may feel productive, but a 200-page manual stored in a forgotten folder does not provide security. It offers only the illusion of preparedness. No one has time to read a novel when a client is waiting or a system is failing.

Bold truth: An SOP that no one uses is not a resource. It is a liability.

Effective documentation is not about dumping information. Strong knowledge systems are designed to be findable, scannable, and integrated into real workflows. Achieving this requires:

- Organizing information by task, not by author
- Using hyperlinks, videos, and decision trees
- Building searchable libraries instead of static PDFs
- Updating content regularly and assigning clear ownership

Many organizations assume documentation exists simply because a checklist or SOP was created at some point.

In practice, documentation must remain active, visible, and relevant. Without those qualities, it becomes a **false sense of security.**

The Quiet Risk of Knowledge Hoarding
One of the most telling signs of an unhealthy culture is knowledge hoarding. In some teams, being the only one who knows how to do something is perceived as job security.

In reality, it is **intellectual gatekeeping** and a **cultural red flag.**

People often hold tight to information not out of malice, but out of fear. The unspoken question becomes: *If I share this, will I be replaced?*
Over time, this creates a silent tradeoff: control in exchange for fragility.

Bold truth: If knowledge is power, then hoarding it becomes a form of control. That behavior does not build resilience; it creates organizational vulnerability.

High-trust cultures normalize documentation, shared ownership, and teaching others as leadership. Low-trust cultures treat documentation as a threat to survival. The result is not only a slowdown in team performance but also a trap that limits growth.

What Strong Teams Do Differently
Resilient teams do not rely on memory. They rely on systems. Success requires:

- Creating living documentation that is regularly tested, rather than created once and forgotten
- Embedding explanation into process design so the *why* is as clear as the *how*
- Normalizing knowledge sharing as a performance expectation, not an optional bonus
- Designing offboarding procedures that capture knowledge, not just collect equipment

One leader I spoke with described it perfectly: *"We operate like every role could win the lottery tomorrow. Our job is to make sure the company still runs."*

The Core Truth

Every departure or departmental change is a test. The measure is whether institutional knowledge survives it. A team that cannot function without one person is not demonstrating strength. It is exposing a liability.

Bold truth: People cannot be future-proofed. Processes can.

Begin by asking: *If you left tomorrow, what would we lose?* Then design systems so the answer is nothing.

Consider This

- What knowledge currently exists only in one person's head?

- Where do we rely more on memory or habit than on documentation?

- What prevents us from capturing and updating what we have already learned?

Tacit Rhythm Disappears Signal

You can hire a résumé. You cannot hire rhythm.

Every team has a rhythm, a flow of how things get done that is not always written down or taught explicitly. Many refer to it as tacit knowledge. It lives in shared habits, inside jokes, unspoken norms, and subtle patterns of coordination. A signal appears when the rhythm is disrupted or lost, often after someone leaves. New hires may struggle to "get how things work here," not because they lack skill, but because the flow was never made visible.

The issue extends beyond onboarding. The true question is how well a team has made the invisible visible. When culture and cadence rely only on intuition, turnover inevitably slows progress. Leaders must ask whether ways of working can be learned or whether they vanish with the people who carry them.

Ask yourself: If a new person joined your team tomorrow, what would they struggle to learn, not because it is hard, but because no one teaches it?

Tacit rhythm is the unspoken flow of how a team really operates. It includes routines, instincts, and habits not captured in SOPs but essential for keeping everything running smoothly. When someone leaves, the loss of this rhythm creates confusion, disconnection, or hesitation. The signal forces the question: How easily can your culture carry on?

Every team has someone who carries a particular flow. That person knows which client needs reassurance before signing a contract. They understand the order of steps that work, not just the one written in the standard operating procedure. They anticipate issues before they arise and adapt quickly when conditions shift. This wisdom is not taught; it is built through repetition, mistakes, corrections, and memory. It forms the heartbeat of effectiveness.

When that person departs, the absence is felt beyond their output. The team loses fluency. The organization loses flow. What vanishes is the subtle rhythm that made everything work.

When It Becomes Real
A new hire arrives with a strong résumé and experience that checks every box. On paper, the person appears to be a perfect fit. Within weeks, tasks take longer, questions pile up, and minor issues begin to build. Clients sense a shift, and the team feels like it is compensating. The new employee is not failing, but they are not fluent.

The issue is not technical skill. The missing piece is **rhythm**. The intuitive cadence of how things get done has disappeared.

What the Research Revealed
In interviews, participants shared stories of losing someone who carried tacit knowledge. This knowledge included not only steps or systems, but

also judgment. It reflected years of learning, which rules could be bent, what tone to use with a sensitive client, or how to fix a recurring issue without escalation. These employees were not always the loudest or most celebrated, but their absence created disruptions that were difficult to repair.

One participant explained, *"We thought we were prepared. We had the steps written down. What we didn't have was the thinking behind those steps."* Another added, *"She made the job look easy. Then she left, and it took three people to figure out what she was really doing."*

That is the moment rhythm disappears, and the organization notices.

The Illusion of Replacement

Many organizations assume that if the résumé matches, the results will follow. The assumption is dangerous. It overlooks the reality that employees carry not just skills but instinct, treating roles as interchangeable, risking losing what made a team member uniquely effective.

Bold truth: You can replace a seat. You cannot replace the insight built into the seat.

Some leaders believe their systems are strong simply because documentation exists. In practice, documents rarely explain how exceptions are handled, which mistakes to avoid, or what small adjustments make the difference. The result is a fragile handoff. A new hire may follow every instruction correctly and still fall short.

How Strong Teams Retain Rhythm
Organizations that navigate departures successfully treat rhythm as something to preserve. They normalize the transfer of context, not just tasks. They embed knowledge capture into daily routines instead of waiting until someone resigns. They create training that mirrors real decisions, not just rote instructions.

Examples of these practices include:
- Encouraging employees to explain their decisions during team meetings
- Creating video walkthroughs that capture the nuances of problem-solving
- Hosting "learn by scenario" sessions that extend beyond the rulebook
- Building searchable archives where edge cases and past lessons are documented

The Core Truth
Tacit knowledge transforms good work into great work. It remains invisible yet holds the system together. When it leaves, cracks eventually appear.

Bold truth: Rhythm is not optional. Rhythm is operational.

Systems that depend on individuals carrying unspoken insight are incomplete. Relying on this fragility is borrowing against the future. The loss of rhythm is not simply a personnel issue; it is a structural vulnerability. Employees cannot be prevented from leaving. The goal is to ensure the knowledge they carry does not leave with them.

The strongest teams prepare not only for replacement but for resilience.

Consider This
What invisible routines keep your team functioning smoothly?
Who quietly carries the team's rhythm, and are they aware of that role?

How does flow or momentum shift when someone leaves?

Domain 2: Trust & Team Health

Trust forms the foundation of any resilient team. It creates an environment where people can speak openly, admit mistakes, and ask for help without fear. Team health reflects the overall well-being of that environment, including whether relationships feel respectful, workloads are balanced, and contributions are recognized.

When trust is weak, people begin to protect themselves instead of collaborating fully. Conversations become guarded, feedback is softened or withheld, and small conflicts are avoided rather than resolved. Over time, silence becomes the default response to strain, leaving problems to grow unnoticed.

Signals in this domain: **Emotional Burden Goes Unnoticed** and **Culture & Leadership Gaps Show**, reveal how well the organization supports its people beyond the basic requirements of the job. Strong trust and team health allow for difficult conversations, shared problem-solving, and resilience in the face of change. Weakness here leaves teams vulnerable to burnout, disengagement, and eventual turnover.

Emotional Burden Goes Unnoticed Signal
When someone leaves, they do not just create a vacancy. They leave behind weight, extra responsibilities, unanswered questions, uncertainty, and emotional strain. A signal appears when the emotional burden is not acknowledged or addressed. Even high-performing teams can quietly absorb stress until it turns into burnout, resentment, or disengagement. Often, the pressure shows up not in loud complaints but in silence, hesitation, or chronic overwork. If your system does not allow for checking in, recalibrating, or redistributing the load, people will carry more than they should. The signal highlights how effectively your culture supports emotional honesty, shared responsibility, and care in the face of disruption.

Ask yourself: Who has taken on invisible emotional weight during a transition, and how is that weight showing up in their energy or engagement? When someone leaves an organization, what they take with them is usually tangible, such as tasks, access, and relationships. What remains is less visible but equally heavy: the emotional residue carried by those who stay.

Turnover often creates emotional strain ranging from grief and guilt to resentment or uncertainty. When the burden is ignored or minimized, teams absorb it quietly, leading to burnout or disengagement. The signal measures how well your culture acknowledges and supports people emotionally during change.

The strain may include the stress of uncertainty, the frustration of stretched workloads, and the dread of knowing you may be next to leave or next to absorb more. Burdens rarely appear in dashboards. They show up in tired eyes, skipped lunches, missed family moments, and silent resignation.

Failing to acknowledge the strain is more than a passing inconvenience. It is a signal that emotional weight is being overlooked.

Bold Truth: An employee can be at their desk yet still not be on the mission.

What the Signal Sounds Like
Common phrases that reflect an unnoticed burden include:

- "I'm fine. Just tired."
- "It is what it is."
- "I'll figure it out."
- "It's just been one of those weeks… months… years."

On the surface, these phrases sound like resilience. In reality, they often reflect resignation. The employee has stopped hoping for relief and is bracing for more.

When Emotional Labor Goes Unseen

In research interviews, employees described the emotional cost of absorbing another person's workload without clarity, time, or recognition. One participant explained:

"When my colleague left, I didn't get a conversation. I got a calendar invite for their tasks. That was the debrief."

Another shared:

"I was training the new hire, doing my job, and covering theirs. When I pushed back, my manager said, 'We picked you because you're strong.' But I didn't feel strong. I felt abandoned."

Bold Truth: The stronger they seem, the less likely anyone is to check if they're okay.

The Cost of Emotional Accumulation

An unnoticed emotional burden does not disappear. It compounds. Over time, people become more withdrawn, more cynical, and less creative. They avoid feedback, fear transparency, and begin expecting the worst. The phrase "It is what it is" becomes a defense mechanism.

This is not a strength. It is a coping strategy. Eventually, it develops into what researchers call learned helplessness: the belief that no action will change anything, so speaking up feels pointless.

Bold Truth: Silence at work is often the prelude to a departure.

Leadership Adds or Lightens the Load

Leaders sometimes increase the burden without realizing it. After a departure, they may make statements such as:

- "Well, this wouldn't have happened if Alex had followed the process."
- "She left her team hanging. That's on her."
- "They weren't that great anyway."
- Remarks like these are not just careless. They are signals that leadership prioritizes blame over support. They teach remaining employees one lesson: it is not safe to struggle.

Bold Truth: How leaders talk about someone after they leave teaches employees how safe they are while they stay.

What Good Looks Like

The best organizations do not treat departures as disruptions to ignore. They treat them as opportunities to listen. Healthy responses include:

- Pausing before redistributing tasks
- Holding space for informal check-ins or debriefs
- Normalizing the question, "How is this affecting you?"
- Creating shared rituals of transition, closure, or celebration

- Providing leadership training that builds emotional intelligence and psychological safety

These actions are not soft skills. They are system-level resilience builders.

The Core Truth

Emotional labor is real. So is emotional debt. When people are expected to carry both without recognition or relief, silent attrition follows. The body remains while the mind and heart drift.

Retention requires more than tracking performance. It requires tending to the load.

Bold Truth: The question is not whether your team is carrying extra. The question is whether they believe anyone notices.

Consider This

- How does your team acknowledge or respond to emotional stress during change?

- What emotions go unspoken after someone leaves?

- What assumptions are made about how people should cope?

Culture & Leadership Gaps Show Signal

When someone leaves, the vacancy extends beyond the role. The culture also gets tested. Times of transition often reveal how strong or fragile the culture truly is. The signal focuses on leadership response, communication, and cultural continuity. Do leaders steady the team, live the values, and apply lessons from exits? Or do people feel lost and unsupported?

Ask yourself: When someone leaves, what do people say, or avoid saying, about leadership, and what does that reveal about your culture?

Many organizations pride themselves on being a great place to work. They display values in shared spaces, highlight words like "team," "transparency," and "supportive" during onboarding, and often describe the workplace as a family. The words feel reassuring until disruption enters the room.

When turnover occurs, cracks begin to show. The response, or the absence of one, speaks louder than any framed statement on a wall. Employees pay attention. They observe not only the person who left but also how leadership shows up for those who remain. Do leaders communicate clearly? Do they acknowledge the impact? Do they model calm, compassion, and presence? Or do they dismiss concerns, pressure people to "step up," or act as if nothing has changed?

The signal becomes clear through leadership actions that follow an exit. Truth emerges not in slogans or websites but in meetings, conversations, and moments when employees are watching closely.

Bold Truth: Display values are meaningless if they disappear under pressure.

Signal in Practice
The signal surfaces when leadership behavior during and after turnover fails to align with stated values.

Common signs include:

- Silence from leaders following a departure, especially when the employee was long-tenured or high-impact

- Defensiveness or blame-shifting when feedback points to leadership issues

- Forced optimism, such as saying "everything's fine" when it is not

- Pressure to accept extra work without recognition, choice, or support

- Dismissal of concerns with phrases like "That's just part of the job" or "We all have to carry more now."

- Cultural slogans used to suppress feedback or guilt employees into silence, such as "we're like a family."

The "We're Like a Family" Myth

Organizations often use family language to promote closeness and loyalty. At first, the framing can feel comforting, but it frequently becomes a trap.

When "family" means:

- Always being available regardless of personal cost
- Avoiding questions because challenging authority feels disrespectful
- Staying silent to keep the peace
- Working without boundaries under the idea of "we're all in this together"

It stops being culture and becomes emotional manipulation.

Bold Truth: A workplace that calls itself a family but treats people as disposable is not a family. It is a contradiction.

Healthy workplaces are supportive and also bounded. Loyalty can exist without guilt, and community can exist without co-dependence.

What the Research Revealed

In interviews, employees described seeing a different side of leadership after someone left. Leaders who once seemed engaged suddenly went silent. Some became defensive. Others leaned into control, micromanaging tasks or insisting people "stay positive" instead of allowing honest reflection.

One participant shared, *"After my teammate left, leadership never addressed it. They just reassigned the work like she hadn't been here for 10 years. It made me wonder how they'd treat me if I left."*

Another described feeling pressured into agreement: *"They kept rephrasing the same question until I gave the answer they wanted. That's not feedback. That's pressure."*

Such patterns create psychological friction. Employees realize that speaking up is unsafe, truth-telling carries risk, and leadership behavior does not match leadership words.

The breakdown of trust leads to disengagement, fear, and eventually more exits.

High-Trust vs. Low-Trust Leadership

Leadership Behavior	High-Trust Culture	Low-Trust Culture
Acknowledging the Exit	Transparent and human	Silent or vague
Responding to Feedback	Welcomed and acted on	Ignored or punished
Redistributing Work	Collaborative and thoughtful	Immediate and unquestioned
Explaining Transitions	Honest, with clear rationale	Sugarcoated or avoided
Demonstrating Values	Lived consistently under pressure	Abandoned when inconvenient
Using "We're a Family" Language	Rare, and only when trust is strong	Frequent, often to deflect accountability
Treating Leavers	With respect and gratitude	With judgment or blame

What Good Looks Like

Healthy cultures do not fear turnover. They prepare for it and use it as an opportunity to strengthen the system rather than protect appearances.

Effective leaders:

- Acknowledge the impact of the departure with clarity and compassion

- Avoid sugarcoating or dodging difficult conversations

- Reassure teams that reflection and recalibration will occur

- Create space for questions, grief, and honest input without retribution

- Follow through on feedback and communicate changes transparently

These actions are not about perfection. They are about consistency and psychological safety.

The Core Truth

Culture is not what leaders say. It is what they reinforce in moments of disruption. During turnover, employees watch closely. They watch how leaders speak about the person who left. They notice how leaders treat those who remain. They evaluate whether values are lived in practice or vanish under pressure.

A culture worth staying in is proven not in calm moments but in times of loss. Leadership is tested when someone walks away.

Bold Truth: Leadership that only works when everything is going well is not leadership. It is a theater.

Consider This

- How consistently are values lived out during change or disruption?
- What does exit reveal about leadership strengths or gaps?
- How do your leaders steady the team or add to the turbulence?

Domain 3: Service & Impact

Service represents the quality of delivery to clients, customers, or stakeholders. Impact reflects the organization's ability to fulfill its mission and maintain trust beyond its internal walls. Strong internal systems, healthy teams, and clear communication all influence the external service experience.

When this domain begins to show strain, it often means that earlier problems inside the organization have gone unresolved. Declines in service quality or breaches in client trust are usually symptoms of deeper issues, such as knowledge gaps, poor coordination, or weakened morale, that have now reached the outside world.

Signals in this domain: **Service Quality Suffers** and **Client Trust Fractures** are among the most visible to those outside the organization. By the time they appear, the cost of inaction is high, and recovery requires more than short-term fixes. Addressing these signals protects relationships, preserves reputation, and ensures the organization continues to deliver on its promises.

Client Trust Fractures Signal

When a team member exits, attention often centers on what is lost internally: tasks, knowledge, and routines. Far less discussed is the disruption that occurs externally in the relationships the employee carefully built with clients, customers, and partners. Many times, those relationships carry more weight than the employee's formal responsibilities.

Clients build trust with people, not just brands or systems. When a familiar face leaves, confidence can weaken even if the service continues. The signal reflects how an organization manages continuity in client experience. It shows whether trust is embedded in systems or rests in the hands of individuals. If clients are left feeling unsure, unheard, or disconnected during transitions, the relationship suffers. The impact extends beyond customer service. It is a measure of how well internal processes sustain external confidence. When clients feel seen and supported during change, credibility remains intact.

Consider a client relationship that shifted after someone left. What did it reveal about where trust truly lives?

When a key team member departs, client relationships often weaken. Trust suffers if transitions are poorly managed or if knowledge about client needs is only held in individual memories. The signal evaluates how effectively your systems and culture maintain client trust through change.

The warning signs may be subtle. A client's emails take on a colder tone. A long-time partner stops returning calls. A complaint surfaces about something minor, yet the tone feels different. These are not signs of inconvenience; they signal trust erosion.

Erosion of trust is Turnover Signal 4: Client Trust Fractures. The concern is not just metrics. It has meaning. Once trust breaks, recovery is slow, expensive, and far from guaranteed.

Bold Truth: Trust is built in conversation. It is lost in transition.
Often, the departing employee served as the emotional glue. They understood nuance, translated internal chaos into calm explanations for the client, anticipated needs without being asked, and resolved issues quietly before they escalated. After they leave, no one may be able to name exactly what is missing, only that something feels different.

Story Layer: The Invisible Departures
In research, one participant described losing a seven-year client because the account manager left and the new contact "just forwarded emails." The client felt as if they were starting over with a stranger who had no context for their history, pain points, or preferences.

Another participant described a major client who stopped all contact: no explanation, no complaints, only silence. When leadership followed up, the client responded: *"We trusted the last person. We didn't feel like you cared who replaced them."*

In both cases, the systems failed to convert relational capital into organizational strength.

What's Really at Stake
Clients rarely build loyalty to a brand alone. They build loyalty with people. When the trusted person disappears and the emotional disruption is ignored, clients feel discarded, not briefed, and not reassured. Discarded.
A new hire cannot be expected to "pick it up." Trust is not a task to inherit. It is a feeling to earn.

Bold Truth: A CRM field cannot replace a relationship.

Why the Signal Gets Missed
Organizations often approach client continuity as a logistical checklist:

- "Did we send the intro email?"

- "Did the new person get access to the files?"

- "Did the meeting stay on the calendar?"

Surface-level questions like these miss the more profound need for emotional continuity. Clients want to feel known, not managed.

Often, the employee who left had a deep rapport with the team. They knew when a client needed reassurance, which deliverables were most critical, and how to navigate tension without drawing attention to it. Without that knowledge, a new hire is forced to rebuild trust from scratch while pretending nothing changed.

Clients can tell when they are treated like contracts instead of relationships. A transition handled without empathy or personalization communicates one message: *"We'll assign someone else. You'll be fine."*
Clients are not looking for a fine. They are looking for a connection. Trust fractures begin when they stop believing you care about preserving that connection.

High-trust organizations approach transitions as moments of care, not closure. Clients receive personal briefings, involvement in planning, and space to voice concerns. Low-trust organizations announce transitions with nothing more than a calendar invite.

What Good Looks Like
Organizations that protect client trust through turnover do more than fill roles. They honor relationships by:

- Identifying high-trust accounts long before turnover occurs

- Sharing institutional memory through living client profiles
- Co-owning relationships across roles to avoid single points of failure
- Involving clients in transition planning rather than notifying them afterward
- Preparing replacements with nuance, not just task lists
- Having leaders personally thank clients for their patience and partnership

Clients who experience thoughtful handoffs gain trust. They come to see your organization not only as responsive but as reliable.

Bold Truth: If a client is loyal to one person and not to the system, the organization is fragile, not strong.

The Long-Term Risk
Once trust fractures, clients rarely complain. They simply disengage. By the time a contract ends or a renewal goes unsigned, the decision to move on has already been made. The opportunity to repair the relationship is gone.

Every unacknowledged transition plants a seed of doubt. Over time, those seeds grow into distance and eventually departure. Many organizations never fully understand why.

The Core Truth

Client trust is never automatic. It is an asset earned through attention, consistency, and care. When someone a client trusts leaves, the transition must be handled with the same care as any external campaign or internal strategy.

Turnover is not only an internal disruption. It echoes outward. If you do not watch how it affects client relationships, you are solving only half the problem.
Strong organizations never assume trust will transfer. They ensure it.

Consider This

- What systems or habits ensure continuity when a key contact changes?

- What details do clients expect us to remember, and where are they stored?

- How does turnover affect client confidence, even in subtle ways?

Service Quality Suffers Signal

Turnover often creates invisible pressure on performance. Even when teams are doing their best, the loss of a key contributor can strain capacity, delay responses, or lower the overall standard of service. The signal measures how well an organization maintains quality when someone exits. The concern is not only about catching mistakes but also about whether systems are designed to support consistent delivery under stress. If service excellence depends entirely on individual effort, turnover will always put outcomes at risk. The signal invites leaders to examine how their teams preserve quality, adapt under strain, and protect the experience of those they serve, even during transitions.

Ask yourself: What is one way service delivery quietly suffers after a turnover, even if it was not noticed right away?

When a key team member leaves, the immediate concern is usually coverage. Who will take on their responsibilities? How quickly can a replacement be hired? Lost in this scramble is a more subtle cost: the steady decline in service quality.

Even when no complaints are voiced at first, customers notice the difference. Emails take longer to answer. Deliverables arrive with minor errors. Support feels less responsive. At first, the changes may seem minor. Over time, they erode overall service quality.

Bold Truth: Turnover is not just an internal disruption. It becomes an external liability when clients begin to question your consistency and competence.

The signal rarely arrives loudly. It appears in delayed responses, in clients copying more people on emails, and in complaints that sound sharper than usual. Those early signs are small fractures that widen when ignored.

The Moment It Becomes Real
A client sends a follow-up because the original request was missed. A new team member is responsible for a deliverable but lacks context about the client's preferences or expectations. The response arrives late. The tone feels off. Trust begins to weaken.
The team, already stretched thin, continues to work hard. Despite the effort, the service now feels reactive, inconsistent, and less reliable.

One participant explained:
"We were still getting things done, but the quality wasn't there. And honestly, the clients noticed before leadership did."

In interviews, the same pattern emerged repeatedly. Clients felt the impact of turnover before leadership acknowledged it. Service timelines slipped.

Communication decreased. Deliverables arrived late or with errors.

Many teams described feeling immense pressure to maintain performance without additional resources. The result was silent overwork, quick fixes, and eventually, client dissatisfaction.

Bold Truth: Service quality does not erode because people stop caring. It erodes when the system expects full output from a partial team without adjustment.

Another participant said:
"Clients didn't know someone left. They just saw the errors. They didn't care why it happened. They just knew it shouldn't have."
Clients are not interested in excuses. They are interested in consistency. Once that slips, even temporarily, the relationship is damaged.

When Hero Culture Makes Things Worse
In many organizations, the default response to turnover is to rely more heavily on the most reliable people. High performers step in to cover the gaps. Their extra effort may keep things afloat temporarily, but it is not sustainable.

Bold Truth: Hero culture is not a resilience strategy. It is a warning sign that the system relies on over-functioning instead of preparation.

Even heroes have limits. When they reach them, the fallout is even greater.

Pretending Nothing Happened

Leaders often try to project confidence and control during transitions. While stability is important, ignoring the pressure on the team sends the wrong message. It signals to employees that their extra effort is both expected and invisible. It signals to clients that nothing has changed, even when the quality has.

Bold Truth: Saying "we're fine" when you are not fine does not build trust. It breaks it.

Clients are often more understanding than leaders expect. They want transparency and reassurance, not silence or avoidance.

What Good Looks Like

Organizations that maintain service quality during turnover do not try to mask the strain. They plan for it, communicate through it, and provide their teams with room to recover.
They:

- Inform clients of transitions and introduce new contacts early

- Adjust timelines and expectations when needed

- Build in quality assurance support during high-risk periods

- Allow breathing room for teams, even if it means slowing down temporarily

These actions send a clear message: We value quality, we value our people, and we are committed to earning your trust, even during disruption.

The Core Truth
When turnover occurs, the impact is felt beyond internal processes. Clients think so as well. They may not always say something directly. Many do not. Instead, they quietly adjust their expectations, question your dependability, and begin exploring other options.

Bold Truth: Service quality is not only a client concern. It reflects the culture of how your organization handles change, pressure, and care.

A strategy built on silence, speed, and sacrifice may hold temporarily. Eventually, quality slips and trust slips with it.

Authentic leadership acknowledges the cost of change, prepares for its impact, and protects the people and partnerships that make the organization work.
Turnover does not have to derail service. The danger comes only when leaders pretend nothing has changed.

Consider This

- What is the first thing clients notice when someone leaves?

- Where are we most reliant on individuals to maintain quality?

- How does your team stabilize performance under pressure?

Domain 4: Systems & Support

Systems provide the structure for how work gets done. Support ensures those systems function reliably under real-world conditions. Together, they form the operational backbone of the organization. When systems are weak or inconsistent, work depends on individual heroics instead of reliable processes. Employees spend energy creating workarounds, patching problems, or compensating for gaps that should have been addressed through design. Support failures, whether in tools, training, or leadership alignment, add unnecessary friction and frustration.

Signals in this domain: **Broken Systems** and **Cross-Org Misalignment Surfaces**, highlight where the organization's infrastructure is under strain. Addressing these signals means more than fixing a single tool or process. It requires creating resilient systems that can adapt to change without disrupting operations or overburdening people. Strong systems and dependable support free teams to focus on meaningful work rather than constant problem-solving.

Broken Systems Signal

Organizations often claim they have "systems in place." In practice, this may mean a shared SOP folder, a checklist, or access to a tool such as a ticketing platform. Having tools, however, is not the same as having support. Many so-called systems are not truly systems at all. They are a patchwork of outdated documents, informal workarounds, and processes that function only because someone props them up.

Bold Truth: A system is only as strong as its ability to function without the hero who built it.

When someone leaves, the illusion of structure collapses. What once appeared to be a process turns out to have been a person.

A carefully maintained Tool might have lived only on their desktop. An onboarding plan may be outdated and irrelevant. Administrative support that kept operations running might have been quietly absorbed by managers who were never trained to handle it.

The signal exposes the hidden burden that broken systems place on teams. People spend their days patching holes instead of doing meaningful work. When tools are slow, they build spreadsheets. When support disappears, they absorb the gap. Instead of preventing problems, they improvise through them, all while hoping not to drop the ball.

Bold Truth: Tools that are outdated, disorganized, or ignored do not support performance. They drain it.

The cost is more than operational drag. Employees become discouraged, under-resourced, and unseen. They stop raising issues because they believe no one will listen.

Over time, they burn out or leave.
Breakdowns like these do not reflect employee failure. They reveal infrastructure failure. When a system demands over-functioning just to maintain the status quo, that system is already broken.

Bold Truth: Peak performance cannot be expected from people navigating friction at every step.

What the Signal Looks Like in Practice
A frontline employee manages customer support through an outdated ticketing system that lacks note sharing or escalation. To cope, they create a personal spreadsheet that no one else can interpret.

An onboarding checklist exists, but it has not been updated in years. It includes irrelevant steps and omits crucial ones. New hires feel confused and overwhelmed from day one.
After an administrative staff member leaves, their responsibilities are redistributed across managers. Senior leaders suddenly juggle travel, scheduling, and budget coordination, none of which fall within their roles or capacity.

Employees repeatedly request process improvements or updated tools. Leadership delays action, insisting, "What we have works well enough." In truth, it only works because people bend over backward to compensate.

Instead of focusing on strategic work, team members spend hours fixing preventable errors caused by outdated systems. Morale drops, frustration rises, and turnover increases.

Bold Truth: Hidden work is not sustainable work. When success depends on workaround experts, the system is not scalable.

Resilient Organizations

Resilient organizations never mistake the presence of a tool for the presence of a system. They build infrastructure that is current, accessible, and aligned with how people actually work, not how leaders imagine they work.

Processes are treated as living systems that require ongoing maintenance. Reliance on individual memory or goodwill is avoided. Clarity is embedded into workflows, friction is reduced, and documentation supports continuity, not just compliance.

System feedback is not dismissed as complaining. It is treated as valuable data. Teams are encouraged to name workarounds instead of hiding them. If a custom spreadsheet is necessary for someone to function, the key question becomes: "Why was that necessary?" The goal is not to patch symptoms but to uncover what the workaround reveals about system design.

Resilient organizations revisit onboarding regularly, align tools with real practices, and ensure documentation is searchable, accessible, and updated. When someone leaves, the system bends but does not break.

Bold Truth: Accountability cannot exist in environments that lack structure. Systems must support expectations before enforcing them.

Consider This

- What parts of your workflow function only because someone is quietly fixing them behind the scenes?

- Where are teams relying on shadow systems instead of official processes?

- Which tools or platforms feel outdated but remain in place because no one has had time to replace them?

- Who is taking on responsibilities they were never trained or hired to do?

- What repeated tasks create waste, confusion, or delay?

Cross-Org Misalignment Surfaces Signal

When someone exits the organization, especially from a cross-functional role, unclear ownership and misaligned workflows become visible. The signal measures how well teams coordinate across boundaries. Is there clarity on who does what, how work flows between departments, and how transitions are managed?

Ask yourself: Where do handoffs between teams get messy, and how does that show up more clearly after someone exits?

An exit can uncover misalignments that were previously hidden. Processes that once looked seamless begin to show cracks. Projects stall because ownership is uncertain. Communication breaks down between departments that assumed they were aligned. Conflicting priorities appear. Deadlines shift. Confusion spreads.

The signal becomes clear when turnover exposes that the real issue is not just about losing a person, but about misalignment across teams, systems, and expectations. When connectors leave, the seams of the organization are exposed.

In many companies, individuals unintentionally serve as the glue holding interdependent processes together. They route communication, bridge handoffs, and manage unspoken workflows. Their invisible labor often goes unrecognized. Once they depart, the quiet fixes vanish, leaving visible operational failures.

What the Signal Looks Like in Action
A cross-functional initiative begins to fall apart after a key project manager resigns. Sales believed the launch date was four weeks away. Marketing is expected to go live next week. Engineering was waiting for specs, but no one submitted them. The misalignment had always existed, but the person who left had been smoothing it over with behind-the-scenes coordination.

A customer escalates a complaint. Sales promised one experience, operations described another, and support delivered a third version. Each team believed it was acting correctly, yet no one worked from the same playbook.

Such breakdowns are rarely isolated. They reveal a deeper issue: the absence of shared understanding and consistent collaboration across the organization.

Bold Truth: Misalignment hides behind informal fixes until disruption forces it into view.

The Difference Between Collaboration and Clarity
Many companies claim to promote cross-functional collaboration. They host all-hands meetings, strategy sessions, and departmental check-ins. Without clarity, however, collaboration creates noise instead of progress. Two teams may pursue

the same goal while working on different timelines, with various tools, and with varying definitions of success. The result is parallel silos, not alignment.

Alignment requires more than goodwill. It requires shared systems, a common language, and clearly defined ownership. When these elements are missing, people operate with assumptions instead of agreements. Once a key individual leaves, those assumptions collapse.

What the Research Revealed
In research interviews, participants often described individuals as "the go-to," "the bridge," or "the translator" between departments. These roles emerged informally and were never formally designed. When those individuals left, organizations realized there were no processes to sustain their coordination.

One participant recalled a senior analyst whose work connected data across multiple departments. After the analyst left, teams continued working independently, but the quality and timing of deliverables deteriorated. No one had visibility into the whole process. Silos were not simply a communication issue; they were a design issue.

Bold Truth: If success depends on people coordinating around broken structures, the structure is the problem.

When Misalignment Becomes Culture
Misalignment, when unaddressed, grows into more than workflow issues. It becomes cultural. Teams stop reaching across departments because they expect follow-through to fail. Individuals hesitate to raise concerns for fear of being blamed for systemic problems.

Leadership can reinforce this dynamic when they focus only on departmental wins instead of collective outcomes. Rewarding quick fixes over collaborative problem-solving further deepens the divide. Incentives that encourage teams to protect their turf make alignment nearly impossible.

Resilient Organizations
Organizations that remain strong through turnover design for alignment with intention. They:

- Establish clear ownership for every function and handoff

- Define roles and responsibilities not just within teams but across them

- Facilitate regular alignment meetings with cross-functional representation

- Build shared documentation that reflects how departments interact

- Create feedback loops between interdependent teams

- Involve all relevant departments before making process changes to ensure alignment

- Identify and formally support key connectors who ensure continuity

Such organizations understand that strong systems cannot eliminate friction, but they help people move through it together. They also ensure that more than one person knows how the pieces fit, so no departure leaves the system vulnerable.

Bold Truth: Alignment is not a one-time meeting. It is a daily discipline.

The Core Truth

A resilient and aligned organization requires more than good intentions. Structure, communication, and shared ownership across boundaries are essential. Protecting teams from chaos during turnover means ensuring clarity travels farther than any one person ever could.

Consider This

- What are the most common sources of cross-team confusion?

- How are roles and ownership clarified during transitions?

- Which coordination gaps become visible only under stress?

- Do all departments review process changes before implementation?

Part IV: When Culture Turns Toxic

Toxic culture fuels turnover and quietly harms those who remain long after a colleague has left. While the eight signals affect businesses, toxic culture often sits at the root of inefficiencies. Cultures rarely become toxic overnight. They simmer. They build slowly in the silence after someone speaks up and nothing changes. They grow in the confusion created when expectations shift, but communication does not. They deepen in the glances exchanged across rooms when someone leaves and no one names why.

Toxic culture is not always marked by overt cruelty. More often, it emerges through the accumulation of subtle, systemic breakdowns:

- Hoarding information to protect power or control
- Gossip thrives because direct dialogue feels unsafe
- Prioritizing optics over truth
- Favoritism in stretch opportunities and visibility
- New hires are thrown into the deep end without structure
- A culture of hyper-responsiveness where burnout is rewarded

From the outside, these conditions may look

functional. Teams appear busy, results seem decent, yet inside, trust is eroding.

Many people are quick to blame cultural issues on a single "toxic" person. Human and Organizational Performance (HOP) shows us that people act according to the systems they inhabit. When dysfunction appears, the environment must be examined, not just the individual.

Bold Truth: Toxic culture is not about toxic people. It is about systems that allow harm to go unchecked.

HOP emphasizes studying how systems shape choices, understanding why people act as they do within their context, and treating unexpected outcomes as opportunities for learning rather than as grounds for punishment.
Bold Truth: Blame shuts down curiosity. Curiosity creates better systems.

Spotting Toxic Culture

Leaders often overlook signs of cultural decay:

- People stop asking questions
- Feedback becomes overly optimistic or disappears
- Employees confide in peers rather than managers
- Individuals protect their teams instead of the organization

- "It's not my job" becomes common

Toxicity rarely arrives loudly. It hides in retreat, guarded behavior, and learned helplessness. In a toxic culture, those who remain often feel trapped rather than fortunate. They carry the emotional weight of departures without time to process. They create workarounds for broken systems and lose faith in leadership when patterns never change.

Most critically, they stop speaking up. Silence does not mean they do not care. Silence means they no longer believe speaking up will help.

Bold Truth: Silence is not compliance. It is survival.

The Roots Are Systemic

Toxic cultures rarely grow from a single leader or decision. They develop through patterns such as:

- Lack of clarity on how people should work, behave, and be recognized
- Inconsistent accountability that allows harmful behaviors to persist
- Failure to repair relationships or rebuild trust after conflict
- Leaders who do not model vulnerability, curiosity, or growth

Multicausal thinking and **Human and Organizational Performance (HOP)** are essential here. Toxicity rarely results from one bad choice. It emerges from many factors working together.

Several of the Turnover Signals™ often appear in toxic environments:

- Undocumented Knowledge Gaps Emerge when knowledge sharing feels risky
- Emotional Burden Goes Unnoticed when well-being is not prioritized
- Culture and Leadership Gaps Show when issues go unaddressed
- Cross-Org Misalignment Surfaces when silos become survival strategies

No training program alone can fix a toxic culture. Redesign is required.

When Leadership Fuels Toxic Culture

Toxic culture becomes most dangerous when fueled by those with the most authority. When leadership and ownership model harmful behaviors, the signals of dysfunction multiply. The power imbalance makes it harder for employees to speak up, harder for middle managers to buffer the damage, and nearly impossible for teams to sustain a healthy environment.

Owners and executives often set the tone in ways they may not even realize. Casual remarks in meetings, avoidance of hard conversations, or rewarding overwork can quietly normalize toxic behavior. More damaging are deliberate patterns such as favoritism, public shaming, or silencing dissent.

Bold Truth: When leadership fuels toxicity, the culture becomes a mirror of their choices.

Employees expect leaders to set the standard. When those at the top tolerate or promote toxic behavior, employees learn that silence is safer than honesty. They adapt by disengaging, building workarounds, or leaving altogether.

The cost of leadership-driven toxicity includes:

- Erosion of psychological safety: People stop voicing concerns or new ideas because they fear retaliation

- Burnout disguised as loyalty: High performers push themselves unsustainably, hoping to prove worth in a system that will never give enough back

- Distrust across levels: Promises of "we value our people" ring hollow when leaders act otherwise

- Quiet attrition: Employees stop leaving feedback and simply plan their exit

Bold Truth: Culture cannot be healthier than the behavior of those leading it.

Working in a toxic environment fueled by leadership often creates a painful double bind. Employees want to do good work and protect their careers, yet speaking up risks backlash. They may feel responsible for change they cannot realistically make, leading to guilt, exhaustion, and eventual resignation.

One employee described it this way:
"We kept trying to fix things at our level, but the message from the top was clear. Our effort didn't matter if it didn't match their narrative."

Even when owners or executives contribute to toxicity, small steps can begin shifting the culture:

- Create safe peer spaces for employees to share their experiences

- Collect anonymous feedback and present aggregated themes, not individual complaints

- Use structured tools such as the Turnover Signal Tool™ to reveal patterns without framing them as personal attacks

- Encourage leadership coaching or external facilitation to create accountability

- Connect turnover data directly to business outcomes so leadership sees the cost in terms they value

Bold Truth: Toxic leadership will not change without awareness, accountability, and consequence.

Organizations cannot out-train, out-coach, or out-process their way past leadership-driven toxicity. If the root cause sits at the top, solutions must begin there. Owners and executives must be willing to look in the mirror, invite honest feedback, and act on it. Without that step, every other effort is a temporary patch.

Bold Truth: A culture fueled by leadership toxicity cannot heal until leaders choose to lead differently.

The Connection to Psychological Culture

Psychological culture reflects the shared sense of safety, trust, and respect within a workplace. A healthy psychological culture allows people to speak openly, share ideas without fear, and admit mistakes without risking judgment or retaliation. It is the invisible foundation of resilience, innovation, and sustainable performance.

Toxic culture erodes psychological culture by replacing openness with caution and trust with guardedness. When people feel unsafe to share concerns or challenge the status quo, the cost is not only emotional but systemic. Fear silences feedback. Uncertainty discourages risk-taking. Exhaustion lowers creativity. Over time, employees stop investing their best energy because the environment tells them it is not safe to do so.

Bold Truth: Toxic culture is not only an operational issue. It is a psychological one.

Research on psychological safety shows that teams thrive when members feel secure enough to take interpersonal risks. Toxic environments strip away this security.

- Instead of trust, there is self-protection.

- Instead of collaboration, there are silos.

- Instead of honest dialogue, there is silence.
When psychological culture turns negative, turnover rises. Those who remain may not physically exit, but they disengage. The mind and heart leave long before the badge or login does.

Bold Truth: A culture that feels unsafe is already losing talent, even if employees have not walked out the door.

Beginning the Shift

Shifting a toxic environment requires deliberate action:

- Name the emotional toll of turnover

- Identify where information is being hoarded and why

- Foster psychological safety at all levels

- Use the Turnover Signal Tool to identify patterns across exits
- Listen to employee insights with curiosity instead of defensiveness

The work is not about blaming individuals. The goal is to remove the conditions that sustain dysfunction.

Bold Truth: Systems shape behavior. If harmful behavior keeps recurring, the system must change.

Reflection: Are You (Unknowingly) Sustaining Toxic Conditions?

These questions are not about assigning blame. They are about creating awareness:

- Do people feel safe giving me bad news?
- When someone leaves, do we discuss how it affected the team?
- Do I call out people in meetings to prove a point raised in private?
- Do I blame those who are no longer able to defend themselves?
- Have I promoted or rewarded people who hoard knowledge?
- Do I get defensive when feedback is uncomfortable?
- Do I repeat topics to push my narrative until I achieve the desired outcome?
- Are stretch opportunities and praise distributed equitably?
- Do I notice who stays silent in meetings and follow up?
- Is burnout normalized or even rewarded?
- When mistakes happen, do we look for learning or for someone to blame?
- Do I know what is really happening, or only what I am told?

Toxicity is not always intentional. Ignoring it, however, is always a choice.

Use these questions not to assign guilt but to understand your role in shaping a culture that either supports or suppresses your people.

Bold Truth: If your team has stopped talking, silence does not mean they are fine. Silence means they have given up hope that speaking up will matter. That is not resilience. It is a resignation. And it is your turnover signal.

Part V: Why The Turnover Signal Model™ is Different

Organizations rarely suffer from a lack of cultural data. Engagement surveys, pulse checks, and leadership scorecards can produce endless charts and metrics. The problem is not in the quantity of information—it is in the kind of information gathered. Many traditional tools capture how people feel in a moment but fail to measure the underlying strength of the systems that shape those feelings.

The Turnover Signal Model™ was designed to close that gap. It evaluates the health of an organization across four essential domains: **Clarity & Continuity**, **Trust & Team Health**, **Systems & Support**, and **Service & Impact**, with **Psychological Safety** at the center. This focus ensures leaders can see the earliest signs of strain, even in environments where employees might hesitate to speak openly.

Unlike approaches that wait for disengagement or turnover to confirm a problem, the Turnover Signal Model™ detects issues while knowledge, skills, and relationships remain inside the organization. That means leaders can act while there is still time to prevent damage rather than trying to repair it afterward.

The model's philosophy comes to life in a simple comparison.

Beyond the Umbrella

A common image of "good leadership" is the leader holding an umbrella over their team, shielding them from office politics, communication chaos, or blame culture. Protection of this kind matters, but remains temporary; once the leader is absent or leaves, the storm falls directly on the team.

Umbrella = Reactive defense, dependent on one person.

The Turnover Signal Model™ replaces the umbrella with a house. A solid, well-designed structure ensures protection is built into the systems rather than being dependent on a single leader's effort.

House = Proactive prevention, sustained by the organization's design

Reality Check: When the Problem Is Above You

Not every leader has the authority to fix what is broken at the top. Sometimes dysfunction originates from the very top. Senior leadership decisions, cultural blind spots, or systemic misalignment may exist without corporate buy-in to fix them.

The model still works under these conditions, but the strategy changes:

1. Stabilize your team under the leaks you can control.
2. Detect and document the signals in neutral, operational language.
3. Use "roof-safe" language that frames issues in terms of business continuity, client impact, and measurable risk.
4. Build a microculture of trust and resilience inside your scope.
5. Know when to exit if the leaks threaten to destroy what you have built.

The Hard Truth: If those at the top refuse to change, and the system protects them, the culture won't transform from the inside out. At that point, staying becomes an active choice to protect what you can, for as long as you can.

Sometimes the healthiest move, for you and your team, is to exit before the dysfunction erodes everything you've built.

Why Most Culture Tools Fail

Many organizations collect large amounts of culture-related data, yet fail to gather the information that truly matters. Tools such as annual engagement surveys or quick pulse checks often provide leaders with a false sense of security. Survey results may look stable or even positive, while the culture is already under strain and vulnerable to breakdown. Culture tools fail for several specific reasons.

They Measure Sentiment Instead of System Health

Most culture surveys focus on employee feelings rather than the functioning of the organization. Personal moods can shift daily depending on workload, home life, or small frustrations. An accurate measure of organizational health requires assessing clarity, continuity, trust, and structural support, which remain more consistent and actionable than mood-based data.

They Rely on Candid Feedback in Unsafe Environments

Low levels of psychological safety discourage employees from speaking up. Workers may feel pressure to respond positively to protect the department's image or avoid upsetting leadership. Inflated scores created under these conditions hide fundamental weaknesses and prevent corrective action.

They Provide Information After Damage Has Occurred

Exit interviews and post-turnover reviews reveal issues only once an employee has left. The opportunity to intervene and address the problem has passed, and the organization absorbs the cost in both financial and morale costs.

They Address Morale Without Repairing Systems

Some culture programs respond to strain with perks, team-building events, or recognition campaigns. These initiatives may temporarily lift spirits, but do not address broken systems, misaligned processes, or unclear expectations that continue to cause stress.

They Target Individuals Instead of Infrastructure

Leader coaching, 360 reviews, and performance improvement plans can improve personal skills. However, such interventions rarely address the broader operational or cultural structures that shape behavior across the entire organization.

Culture tools that operate in these ways keep organizations trapped in a reactive cycle. Leaders only respond once problems have already damaged performance and morale. The Turnover Signal Model™ changes this dynamic by detecting early warning signs, revealing system-level weaknesses, and guiding leaders toward proactive redesign that builds resilience before turnover occurs.

How The Turn Turnover Signal Model™ Closes the Gap

The Turnover Signal Model™ solves the weaknesses found in traditional culture tools by focusing on the health of the organization's systems rather than on temporary sentiment or delayed feedback. The model uses structured tools to identify, analyze, and address the root causes of strain before they cause significant damage.

Measures System Health Instead of Mood

The Turnover Signal Wheel™ organizes signals into four essential domains: Clarity & Continuity, Trust & Team Health, Systems & Support, and Service & Impact. This framework evaluates how the organization operates, not just how people feel on a given day. Leaders receive consistent, actionable insights that remain relevant regardless of short-term mood shifts.

Surface Truth in Low-Safety Environments

The Turnover Signal Self-Assessment™ and SigTac

Signal™ Tool use non-blaming, system-focused language that reduces the risk of retaliation and encourages honesty. Employees evaluate patterns and conditions rather than individuals, which makes it safer to report real issues even in environments with limited psychological safety.

Delivers Insight Before Turnover Happens
Signals such as Tacit Rhythm Disappears or Emotional Burden Goes Unnoticed emerge well before someone resigns. The model captures these early warnings, allowing leaders to act while the knowledge, skills, and relationships remain inside the organization.

Drives Structural Change, Not Just Morale Boosts
The SigTac Signal™ Tool moves leaders from symptom recognition to system redesign. Instead of relying on temporary morale boosts, teams redesign workflows, documentation processes, and decision-making structures to prevent the recurrence of the strain.

Targets Organizational Infrastructure
The model shifts the focus from fixing individuals to repairing the systems that shape everyone's work experience. Improvements in clarity, support, and alignment strengthen the entire culture rather than isolating change to a single role or team.

By addressing these five areas, the Turnover Signal Model™ transforms turnover from an unpredictable disruption into a reliable signal of system health.

Leaders gain the ability to detect fragility early, respond effectively, and design an organization that is resilient in both stability and change.

The Turnover Signal Wheel™ in Action

The Turnover Signal Wheel™ is organized into four essential domains that reflect the health and resilience of an organization.

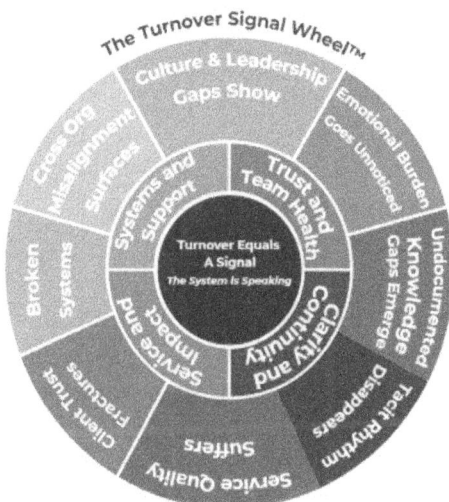

Together, the four categories decode which areas of the organization are under strain and where action is most needed. The framework enables leaders not only to respond to turnover but also to address the root causes it reveals.

For example:

- When Tacit Rhythm disappears, Undocumented Knowledge Gaps are often already present.

- When Client Trust fractures, the cause may lie in earlier missteps involving leadership or cross-team communication.

- When Emotional Burden goes unnoticed, service quality and engagement eventually decline.

The Self-Assessment

The Turnover Signal Self-Assessment™ includes statements tied to each of the eight Turnover Signals™. Participants rate their level of agreement on a 1–5 scale. The goal is not to measure satisfaction or engagement but to listen to the system, identify what is silently working, spot where strain is building, and notice where cracks may soon appear.

The assessment provides a shared, non-blaming language for noticing what would otherwise remain hidden: missing documentation, emotional overload, broken systems, or leadership missteps. It helps teams articulate, "The challenge is not just hard, it is fragile."

Key moments for using the assessment include:

- Before a significant change, restructuring, or growth phase
- During quarterly team health checks or retrospectives
- At leadership retreats, strategy sessions, or offsites
- After an employee departure, it is necessary to reflect on what surfaced and why

Reviewing scores and trends allows leaders to identify which signals are most active and where to focus further attention. Perhaps the data shows strong knowledge-sharing but low emotional safety. Possibly, service quality remains high, but only because one person is silently overcompensating.

Used proactively, the assessment helps organizations intervene before small strains grow into major breakdowns.

Reflection for Leaders

- Where in my organization might cracks already exist that the Wheel could help surface?

- How often do I give my team a safe space to discuss strain before it becomes a problem?

- Am I prepared to act on what the Self-Assessment might reveal, even if it is uncomfortable?

- Do I rely too heavily on individuals instead of building resilient systems?

- What am I willing to change now to protect culture, trust, and long-term stability?

How to Engage

The Turnover Signal Model™ is not designed to live only on the page. Its real power emerges through shared analysis, facilitated dialogue, and collective redesign.

I currently offer workshops, facilitated sessions, and speaking engagements that help leaders and organizations apply the model in real time. These experiences are designed to surface hidden strain, interpret active Turnover Signals™, and guide teams toward practical, system-level improvements.

Engagements may include:

- Interactive workshops applying the Turnover Signal Model™ to real organizational challenges
- Facilitated leadership or team sessions using the Turnover Signal Self-Assessment™
- Keynotes and talks focused on turnover, culture, resilience, and system health
- Guided conversations that translate signals into actionable redesign

Sessions are suitable for leadership teams, conferences, retreats, and organizations navigating change, growth, or transition.

A digital SigTac Signal App™ is in development and will support this work in the future. For now, the focus remains on human-centered application, conversation, and clarity, where the model delivers its strongest impact.

If you are interested in booking a workshop, inviting me to speak, or exploring a facilitated engagement, please reach out directly:

SigTacTure@yahoo.com

Together, we can move turnover from disruption to insight and build cultures designed to endure.

Final Chapter: What Turnover Teaches

Every organization aspires to grow, retain talented people, and build a culture that lasts. Yet change is inevitable. Turnover is one of the most human forms of that change. When someone leaves, it is never just a calendar event or a backfill request. It is a disruption.

The team adjusts, the work continues, and for a moment, the organization holds its breath.
The Turnover Signal Model™ was not created to prevent people from leaving. Departures are a regular part of any healthy organizational life cycle. The model was designed to help organizations recognize what becomes visible when someone departs.

When a team member leaves, they often take more than just tasks or responsibilities. They bring knowledge, rhythm, trust, and insight into the way things work. What remains behind is not just an open role. The absence often exposes areas of the system that depended too heavily on individual effort, personal memory, or silent sacrifice.
The Turnover Signal Model™ provides a way to pause and notice. It introduces a structure for understanding what changed, a language for naming unseen strain, and a set of tools to help teams learn from disruption. Turnover does not just create gaps. It reveals them.

Listening Before the Break

The most significant value of the model often appears before someone leaves. Signals such as emotional burden, client trust erosion, cross-team misalignment, and broken systems tend to surface quietly and gradually. They may appear as missed steps, recurring breakdowns, or unspoken tension long before a resignation.

Leaders are encouraged to listen for those patterns. The Self-Assessment surfaces areas where systems feel strained. The Turnover Signal Wheel™ helps teams visualize how multiple challenges overlap or interact. The tool prompts people to document real events and behaviors, not for blame, but for understanding what the system is honestly asking of its people.

By noticing patterns early, organizations can act with care instead of reacting with urgency. Proactive attention prevents small fractures from becoming full-scale crises.

Culture is not defined solely by what happens when things go well. It is defined by how an organization responds during moments of difficulty and transition. Turnover can test that culture, but with intention, it can also strengthen it.

At the heart of every signal lies psychological safety. Without it, strain remains hidden. With it, teams can speak openly, surface fragility, and respond with resilience.

A Redesign Culture

The most resilient organizations are not those that avoid turnover. They are those who learn from it. They ask not only why someone left, but also what the exit revealed. Instead of rushing to replace, they pause to repair. Departure becomes more than a loss; it becomes information.

A redesign culture focuses on building systems that are supportive and sustainable. It explores where knowledge lives, how emotional burden accumulates, and what structures collapse under pressure.

Organizations move from reaction to reflection, from silence to shared insight.
When people leave, something shifts. That shift can disrupt or transform. The outcome depends on what the organization chooses to do next. The Turnover Signal Model™ offers a way to make that choice with intention.

You are not simply responding to turnover. You are redesigning for what comes after.

If the Roof is Leaking

When "the roof" (senior leadership) is the source of dysfunction, you're in a different game than with the umbrella scenario. Here's how the **Turnover Signal Model™** would frame it:

Stabilize What's Directly Under Your Control
You might not be able to repair the roof itself, but you can reduce damage underneath:
Protect your team from immediate harm by clarifying priorities, creating safe internal norms, and absorbing unnecessary chaos where possible. Shore up weak systems *within* your scope so leaks cause less disruption (e.g., knowledge capture, documented processes, client communication buffers).

Detect & Document Early Signs of Structural Damage
Use the Eight Turnover Signals™ to map the **impact** of the leaks (e.g., increased rework, morale drops, client trust erosion).

Keep documentation fact-based and operational, avoid personalizing or blaming in a way that could be framed as insubordination.

Use "Roof-Safe" Language
Frame your feedback in terms of **business continuity, client outcomes, and risk mitigation**, not cultural judgment.

Example: Instead of "Leadership decisions are harming morale," say "Our rework rate has increased by 27% since X change, and here's the cost impact."

Build a Microculture of Resilience
Create a local environment where psychological safety exists, even if it's absent above.
Focus on retaining *functionality and trust* inside your team; this keeps performance intact and prevents further erosion.

Know When the Structure Is Unsalvageable
If the leaks spread and the corporation refuses to act, the model gives you a clear signal: you may need to move on before the damage undermines everything you've built.

Leaving is not defeat, it's preventing the collapse from taking you with it.

Call to Action for Leaders

Commit to one meaningful conversation this month where you ask, "What is not working for you right now?" Listen without defense. Let the answer guide your next decision. Small acts of curiosity and care are where redesign begins.

Treat the Turnover Signal Model™ not as a one-time tool, but as a rhythm for maintaining organizational health in every season. Use it in stability to stay strong, and in disruption to grow stronger. Turnover is not the end of the story. It is the moment you decide how the next chapter of your culture will be written.

Appendix

Leadership Self-Assessment

Use this self-assessment as a mirror. Not to judge yourself, but to understand what it feels like to be led by you.

- Do I make space for people to disagree with me, without fear of fallout?

- When someone leaves, do I acknowledge the loss or quietly bury it?

- Am I more focused on optics or outcomes?

- Have I ever retaliated (directly or indirectly) against someone for telling the truth?

- Do I walk the culture I claim to build?

- Do I know how people truly feel about working here, or only how they act in meetings?

- When was the last time I asked someone what was not working and then acted to change it?

www.ingramcontent.com/pod-product-compliance
Lightning Source LLC
Chambersburg PA
CBHW071603200326
41519CB00021BB/6849